TRAMP

Barataria Poetry
Ava Leavell Haymon, Series Editor

for Kirk

for Katie, Andrew, and Erik

CONTENTS

A MAN MISTREATED ADA JONES
AND SHE IS SEEKING HIM

Women Flocked to the Municipal Court Today
to Hear 19-Year-Old Boxcar Vagabond Tell Her Story

Most girls wouldn't like this sort of life.

I went to high school two years, read books
of adventure—
                Kidnapped, Sailing Alone,
Farthest North—
                        pulled them off the shelves
with the tips of my fingers,
                        crawled into a boxcar,
stayed there until I was far from home.

My first employer was a young man,
in Kansas City. He took pictures,
portraits in people's homes—
                        women
holding babies, women surrounded by children,
mothers and sisters, backs straight as chairs.

I collected the money. Sometimes I posed.

It is for him I've searched all over the country.
It is a matter of some urgency.

                        I left the baby
with a friend. My father—he wouldn't take him in.

I traced the man to Denver, from there to Chicago,
where I was going when I was arrested.

I've painted buildings, scrubbed floors. Once
I worked in the fields.

            The fun of tramping,
the excitement of never knowing
where you're going, the comradeship—

all of it appealed to me so strongly I almost forgot
the object of my travels—

                        Look at my hands.

Clyde Dixon (I)

Smoke and ash, vinegar and salt, some awful tang
that felt like metal against teeth, did some

breeze blow through, some rain, a flash of cut hay
or blinding snow, a green so wired and flamed she stood

in the door, looked over the bridge as if the river
were a long braid, a tug on the scalp, a satin sash cinched

tight at the waist— Doors slamming shut, slamming
open, lanterns swinging down the tracks, nothing

like paper lanterns she lit when she was a girl, or living
in the woods, some shack on a rented piece of land, lanterns

meant guns, meant dogs, meant someone's lost
or going to get hung— Did she fight the idea the lights

were almost pretty or were they just a way to mark time,
measure space, sign of a town, a house, something to eat?

Bodies of Evidence (I)

A huntsman's dog found a woman's body
just off the highway near the Wakefield line.
The body has not been identified.

∿

Where do I ride?
                 Why, every place.
In the West I can even go in passenger trains,
tell the conductor I'm broke and he'll just walk along
and there I sit on the velvets, big as those
paying six cents a mile.

∿

Walter Locke, whose dog drew him to the place,
found the body to be warm and blood oozing
from six wounds to the head. Five of these
were from pistol bullets. The sixth, which had gashed
the left ear and plunged deep into the neck, was made
by some sharp instrument.

∿

    Sometimes
    I'd sweep houses, do chores,
    pack goods, things like that.

        Sometimes I'd shovel coal.
    The fireman would say, *Hey, kid, want a smoke?*
    I'd say real low, *Aw, naw, I don't smoke.*

        Sometimes, I couldn't find anything.

∿

There was every indication the murder
had been committed elsewhere and the body
dragged from a wagon to the field where it was found.

~

Two Indians came along in a Ford.
They saw me washing. They stopped and fixed breakfast.
We rode on. The one got off somewhere, but the other,
he showed me the town.
                                        Yes, we made love. I liked him.

~

From the number of wounds, authorities believe
the crime was done in anger. The dress
of the woman, the fact she wore two skirts,
three pairs of stockings, and two coats
all seemed to indicate a person well prepared
for long journeys in all sorts of weather.

Postcard

Union Pacific Transfer Depot, Council Bluffs, Iowa

One day you wake up in a town you can't name
and there's no way to plot a path from A to B.
You hear a train, then you don't, the sound

bounces off the hills, gets trapped in a gulley
or skims a church spire only to scatter
over a silo that dreams of nothing but thunder

and grain. Who says the route is not the shortest distance
between two points, says it's a branching river
and you must get in your little boat and paddle

down each grassy inlet and tiny stream—as if sets
of unreadable alphabets opening beneath your feet
and clambering over fence posts were a good thing?

I don't want to come to the edge of myself, don't
want that sinking towards a bottom that never seems
to come. Sometimes I'm held together with pins

and strings. I'm pieces of fabric, a dress waiting
to be seamed, or I'm the stitches ripped out, threads
blown across the floor. I want to lie on a cool, clean

sheet, feel it drape over my face, arch my back
like a cat, be reduced to nothing but bone,
the big wind that races across the field, bend

the trees back, push clouds, be shadow, whip past
blouses hanging on the line like women waiting
for their lives, all of it silver and into the sun.

Dictionary

Big O/Skipper
train conductor

Blinky
rider with one eye

Brakie/Shack
brakeman

Bull
railroad police

Card Man/Woman
hobo with I.W.W. card

Coal Passer/Tallowpot
fireman/stoker

Gandy Dancer
railroad worker

Ghost
beggar

Haybag/High Heels/Road Sister
woman hobo/tramp

Clyde Dixon (II)

Did she lock the door, say goodbye, did she know
when she'd next brush her hair, wash her face?

When she stood before a cool bowl of water, held
her breast, the hollow where her arm met her side,

unwound a roll of gauze, cotton webbing, a bolt
of cheap muslin, what her mother used to pattern

a dress, did she turn in the mirror, double-check—
Stand back. Take measure. Did she look

like a boy? She found the good scissors. She tore
at the gaps in the weft. How short was her hair?

Did she resent what she did and was going
to do and who and what made her do it or did she

not care, did she try not to—she liked it—did she
think for one second she could be free?

Newsbreaks

Lucille Murphy is in the County Hospital mending up some broken bones received from a boxcar fall. She tramped California, working as a messenger boy in El Centro, a bartender in Calexico, and a baggage man in Fresno. She picked corn in the Imperial Valley and sawed wood in the Los Angeles woodyard. Hers is not an isolated case.

~

Dolly Loud is in the Imperial County Jail with three young men under the charge of committing a series of holdups near Jacumba Springs. Her diary contains a history of her wanderings from Los Angeles to San Francisco and back with a companion named Dorothy and another named Eleanor. She notes working in canneries and being frequently broke and hungry. In her diary she wrote, "I'm going to San Diego with Casey, Dick, and Red. I'll probably get into trouble, but here goes nothing."

~

The "woman hobo" may arrive within the next few years, but we don't think so. Woman's inherent regard for personal adornment, if nothing else, stands in the way of itinerant wanderlust. Days and days without mirror, without powder, without time or place to put up the hair—impossible. The "woman hobo" is an extravagant prediction and a myth.

In Her Other Life: Greta Sorensen

If she put her hand in water, if she spread her fingers out, if she caught her own reflection, if she got wood for the fire, water for the stove, did she see a redbud blooming, purple branches bobbing, lanterns in the wind, did she fill her pockets with small, smooth stones, did she know loosestrife, know cornflowers, did she know silt seeping into her shoes, did someone reach in, try to turn the baby, did someone raise her leg, give her a wooden spoon, what was rain, what was snow, did someone say *push,* if she stood against a wall, was it only to wait her turn, did the pain billow like a tent, flare like summer hay, and the clocks, did they stop, the piano ambled on, did she think a body could split itself in half and the past was just the past, a dog a dog, what was all the rushing and blood on the floor, did someone wash the body, did someone straighten the limbs, or was the baby wide-eyed or sleepy and trundled out the door, what about the tilt and twist of the sun, was it the pull of a stitch, the torque of a chain, one hoop inside the other, the thread was cotton or silk, the hoops were birch, they grew by the river, they bent like girls, did she ever walk in?

"HIKING NELL" FACES
THE AUGUST MAJESTY OF THE LAW

—Varied and Vivid Experiences—
While Youth has Played Havoc with "Nell,"
Her Pedestrian Qualities Remain Unimpaired

REPORTER ONE:
Pasco, Wash.—After walking 1,300 miles on a wager of $5,000
to be arrested and forced to spend 60 days in the King County jail
just two weeks' journey from her coveted goal:

REPORTER TWO:
this and even more is the grievance of Nellie Hale,
alias "Hikin' Nell," who was arrested by Officer Torrent
Tuesday afternoon.

REPORTER ONE:
In company with three tramps,
Nell was found in a small tie house busily engaged
preparing a mulligan stew.

REPORTER TWO:
Without protest she accompanied the officer to the city jail
and the following day was given a hearing before Justice McCarthy.

NELL HALE:
(*Takes off hat.*)
I don't want no comment cast my way for I am nothing but a tramp
walkin' my way on a bet from Florida to the Pacific coast.

REPORTER ONE:
Nell answered the chief's questions rapidly and seemed to take
the whole matter as a joke until W. J. Davis appeared with his camera
and attempted to take a picture.

REPORTER TWO:
Nell immediately protested.

NELL HALE:
You make your living and I make mine, but I help you make yours—

REPORTER ONE:
It was not until a hat was passed and the promise given that

NELL HALE:
the whole bunch of us will be shot together

REPORTER ONE:
that she consented to have her picture taken.

REPORTER TWO:
The newspaper fraternity, together with the distinguished court
and officers of the law lined up as per agreement, and the heroine
of many "hikes" was, for the first time, the victim of a camera.

(*Nell puts on hat, checks self in mirror. Flash of light to suggest photo.*)

NELL HALE:
Yes, Judge, if you will let me go, I will hike mighty quick.
It does seem a funny thing that I should start from Pascolia
and wind up in Pasco. Ain't that terrible luck?

Postcard

Monongahela R.R. Passenger and Freight Station,
West Side, Morgantown, W.Va.

Thistle and spur,
the fields are swallows
that bank

through my blood,
they are ice
on my back,

river-wrecked
weeds—they turn
my spine to ash—

I can't tell you
where I am.
I want to sit on a roof

above a run
of goldenrod, dangle
like a bride's earring,

a shoe from a heel—
O keel and swerve,
you startle

and furl, wind-bent
and speed—you
empty my heart.

Dictionary

Jungle
makeshift encampment

Original Ham & Eggs Route
Oberlin, Hampton & Eastern Railroad

Punk and Plaster
bread and butter

Reefer
refrigerated car

Ride the Blinds
sit between the engine and mail/baggage car

Ride the Bumpers
sit on couplings between cars

Ride the Cushions/Ride the Velvets
sit inside a passenger car

Take Your Parcels & Walk
Texas, Pacific & Western Railroad

To Hell & Back
Toronto, Hamilton & Buffalo Railroad

Clyde Dixon (III)

Were there other women, some place to hide, or her back
against slats, she thought *play along, stop time,*

locked herself in a box so when it was over she could
take herself out, a dress folded and pressed, creased

by the weight, the pull of the straps— What would happen
if she bit a cheek, ripped an ear, reached for a bottle

and smashed someone's head—would that make them
stop or just do it harder, splay her legs, jam a dirty hand,

laugh and spit with the others to show what they'd do—
And if she scraped the inside of her thumb, pricked

her fingers till they bled, is that how she checked, knew
she was there, or did she think of her body as separate,

a container, something she divides—how she'd accuse anyone,
say anything if it meant saving her lily white skin—

Reenie Patterson Talks to the Press
about Her Time on the Road

I was helping my dad milk, and I was getting pretty cocky.
I thought as long as I had to work like a man,
I ought to talk like one.
$\qquad\qquad\qquad\qquad$ And so,
one night I started to milk my cow and she swatted me in the eye
with her dirty tail and I got up and whopped her one with my stool
and cussed her out and my daddy came across like a wind
and hit me up one side of the face and down the other.

I said I'd leave home.
$\qquad\qquad\qquad\qquad$ He said I'd be back for supper.

And there was this girl, Eileen, and she wanted to go to Issaquah.
She asked me to go along.
$\qquad\qquad\qquad\qquad$ I thought that was a grand idea.

$\sim$

Of late there has been an increasing number of maverick girl tramps. They
follow the boys, living in jungles and boxcars. They wash clothes, patch
pants, and tidy up the places where both sleep. Occasionally, two girls
attach themselves to a gang of boys and they travel for weeks in peace and
friendship. Others go from jungle to jungle, boxcar to boxcar, any place there
are men or boys. They enter a boxcar or a jungle—and without more ado the
line forms to the right.

$\sim$

Detectives—railroad detectives—were patrolling with lanterns
and rifle up and down the tracks.
$\qquad\qquad\qquad\qquad$ But when the train started,
when it jerked loose,
$\qquad\qquad\qquad$ this whole group rose up and rushed
that one door. I was the first one there and somebody
picked me up by the seat of my pants and pitched me in.

It was absolutely full of men and it was evening and the sun
was setting and we sat in the door and I was swinging my legs.
A man slapped my shins,

> *Hey, girlie, keep your feet down.*
A switch'll jerk you right off, right into eternity.

ᘐ

One afternoon in September, near a city in the grain belt, two girls entered
a jungle where thirty or forty men were cooking mulligans. The girls
helped out with the meal, washed tins, and tidied camp. Then they made a
proposition. There was a boxcar on the tracks nearby. If a man had money,
a nickel or a dime would be appreciated because one of the girls needed
shoes. If not, the man could come anyway, but in lieu of cash, he must help
prepare the girls' supper which they declared should be ready by six o'clock.
All afternoon the girls received the men and boys in the boxcar. Some men
doubled back and repeated. Others visited both girls. Promptly at six o'clock
the girls quit, demanding their supper. They divided their seventy cents in
cash and caught a night-freight east.

ᘐ

Napa, Idaho, August 3rd

Dearest Mom,
Just a line to let you know I'm okay.
The police picked up Eileen and me last night.
They put us in a cell. We sure made use of the cots.
I hope they turn us loose soon so we can go again.
This is the third time they've picked us up.
They think we're runaways.
Fooled, eh?

ᘐ

We got into Soda Springs on Saturday night.
The Henry Stampede was in full swing.

I didn't know

when we left home

Eileen was pregnant.

I don't know how she carried that baby,
the tumbles we took and the way we lived and how we ate.

It's a miracle to me she carried that baby.

༄

On a freight pulling south a skinny little girl of sixteen left the company of
three boys in a reefer for a boxcar of older males. All night she entertained
them. At a water stop, other men, having heard the good news, rushed
forward to the car. By morning every man on the train knew who and what
was in the Chesapeake and Ohio car next to the load of lumber. Two of us,
fearing the child might be murdered, complained to the brakie. In the cold
light of early dawn he went to the car and demanded the girl. She came to
the door a little bit drunk and very undressed. "You big fat fool. You YMCA
dummy. Why do you have to spoil it all? Why can't you let a girl alone when
she isn't hurting you?" The brakie made her ride in a car by herself. From
the door of this car, however, she talked to the men on top. At the first
opportunity she dropped from the train—and two dozen men followed her.

༄

Eileen started a relationship with a cowboy.
Some men like it when a girl's like that.

I told her,
let's go, and she said she was going with the boys to Sun Valley,
to the next rodeo, I should go.

I said no and got a ride with a couple of maniacs.

They tore down that canyon and up behind a hotel. They said,
you go to room so-and-so, we'll be back.

When I got around
that corner, I ran as fast as I could to hunt a freight out of there.

On the Origins of Trampdom: Nell Hale

She never says why she left, what particular thing
set her off—maybe he leaned in too close with his cigar,

maybe he seemed to deliberately let the ash
graze her hand, maybe one night after he climbed

on top of her, after she mixed the alum and water,
lay in the tub and inserted the tube, she knew

she didn't want his child again. If that was it—
she would only say there was a "family tragedy,"

that he beat her, that he did it almost every day—
if they lost a child, if he blamed her and she blamed him,

if he was too cheap to call a doctor, if she wouldn't
let anyone near, if they had to pry the child

out of her arms before the rigor set in, if he thought
hitting her would let her see what she had become,

if one thing led to another and not one plate was left and grief
became a forest they couldn't leave, just the same trees,

the same river, the same outcrops of rock—maybe
she told him about a wedding, a cousin he never met,

she knew the way, her father had shown her how, she packed
five days of skirts and waists, the perfect gift, a tea kettle—

something they'd need—and he took her to the station,
the box wrapped in paper and string, how she let him help her

up the step, how she half-smiled from the train window, the pot
on her lap, how she would use it to wash her face, wash

her hair, cook her dinner, clean her knife, how she turned
and half-smiled, how she turned and looked straight ahead.

Bodies of Evidence (II)

The body of a woman was found about 75 feet
from the west end of the Union Depot platform.
She was lying upon her face, and the only sign
of injury was a deep scalp wound, such as
might have been caused by a blow or severe fall.

My six-shooter?
          It's to ward off any men
who might become too familiar. I've never
used it once, though, and I've been traveling
for almost three years since I broke away
from home with its dances, parties,
and nothing-else-to-do life.

Police Captain Bossung, Louisville, Kentucky

The women tell tales of suffering that are,
for the most part, made up,
                    but one cannot help
but admire the ingenuity of the tellers.

We expect more of them this year.

I got tired of working out in people's kitchens,
the smell of pots and pans.

One day I noticed an account about two women who were walking
on a wager from San Francisco to New York.

Here it was I decided to become a "woman tramp."
I did not confide my resolution to anyone.

⟳

Dr. Mary Hoffman Jones, New York City Municipal Lodging House

I always think I am listening to the story
of a mistake.

The rule is no one is allowed a night's lodging
who has more than 25 cents.

                         It is quite safe to say
they do not come here because they wish.

⟳

I topped a freight train across the Arizona desert.
I was thrown off more trains than I can remember.
I was taken for a German spy.

I found the American man
to be considerate, courteous, and not in the least disposed
to take advantage of my helplessness.

⟳

Miss Genevieve Alexander, who recently tramped
across the continent, is dead, a victim of the influenza.
The knapsack she carried from the Pacific Coast
lay in one corner of her room while her coat hung over
a chair. In the inside pocket was a note from her mother:

Every day I think of you and wish that you were coming home.

Postcard

The Three Bridges on Ohio River
between East Liverpool and Steubenville, Ohio

Don't worry, I promise,
it won't last long.

They take one leg,
then the other, and hold you

on the table until their job
is done. I wouldn't lie,

it hurts, the way they pry
you open with their needles

and crooks, but if you sink
into your body and lie

in the shallows
where fish weave

between muddy grasses
like straw from a broom,

time will pass. They snap
their black bags. Silt

clings to your hair,
the marshy ropes want

to pull you back down,
and lilies float like clouds

whose anchored tails
will tangle you with their lies

and admire your clothes filling
like a flag. I would come to you

if I could in the green spill
of leaves. Stay with me here.

Clyde Dixon (IV)

Did she think about sleep, newspaper blankets, the ink
on her sleeves, did she sing ballads, say phrases—

which way shall I fly, wild above rule or art, arise,
enormous bliss— Would she wade into the river,

wring out the dust, the urine streaking her hem,
she was so thin her period stopped or she needed cotton

or wool—she was a boy—the pennyroyal she used
to make a pregnancy stop— Dry, puffed

in the mouth, she gathered flaked hooves, dung clotted
with grass, baskets-full she sold to tanners, cigar ends

she could trade, did she see milk on the porch, clothes
she could glean or she went round back, peddled needles

and thread, matches or pins, the woman at the door, how did
she look—her hands, her hair, a nest sticky with seeds—

Jail House: Interview

Nell Hale

I would like to know why I am here.

All I did was walk along the street.

I will never tell my right name.

                        No, I do not want
a cigar. I am the daughter of a prominent railroad man
and I prefer cigarettes.

                    I do not mind saying
I am a skilled performer on the piano.

I was reared and educated in Atchison, Kansas.

I married a man in St. Joseph, Missouri. He thinks
I'm dead. He will never know otherwise.

                           I love
this roaming life.

          I beg food.
                    No, I don't work for it.
I was struck by a train.

No, sir, I do not beg money. I have not had money
of my own for a long time.

                    No, I never had any
trouble. I find people good to me wherever I go.

You're one of those newspaper reporters, aren't you?

No, no, I don't want to talk to you.

Thinking of Heaven: Greta Sorensen

If she stood at the edge of the loft, walked herself up those painted stairs, if
she pushed the church doors open and the hooks were empty and the robes
hung like notes in the hall, if the floor creaked and the window behind her
quit the stars like a heavy moon, if she stood at the rail in her too-tight
shoes, pulled in her breath, let it dive deep in her belly, it was so cold, she
trudged through the snow, if she stood there and looked across that expanse
as if she were standing in the prow of a lost ship and the pews were waves
under a roofless sky, if she let herself fall back in the water and the music
did not ruffle and the organ stayed still, her hair rippling under water so she
could be saved, did she think about pushing her voice out of her body, letting
it ride itself out, would she hold onto a hymnal, did she love all the singing,
did it set forth a mighty sound, would she look across the church into the
face of God, she was underwater, *in my father's house are many mansions,*
did she lift a piece of ice from the trough and hold it up like a mirror, was
heaven an endless field of empty snow?

Diagnostics

Hazel Davis

I've had the gypsy strain far back
as I can remember.

        My father gave me
all the advantages of education, but I can no more
resist the lure of the road than I can resist
the desire to live.

        And life is sweet, I assure you.

          ◦∿

from *"Two Souls in One Body: A Psychiatric Case,"* William Lee Howard, M.D., *1905*

The body and mind that friends call woman may at certain periods break
from home and as a tramp or lewd person wander abroad with no realization
of its personality; then after weeks or months, it will return to its other self,
its publicly accepted form, with no recognition of its past self, the ambulant
female hobo.

          ◦∿

I ran away from an old southern seminary
where I was sent to complete my education.
I grew tired of their ways, and one night
after the girls were asleep, I ran away.

A freight train was standing in the yards.
I climbed into an empty car and soon
the lights from town disappeared.

          ◦∿

You cannot, from a scientific viewpoint, say she is insane during these periods, for each is a distinct personality sane in itself. Which is the true self? You would be inclined to say the one of goodness and morality, but may not this be an artificially developed personality and the real one is the one in which she reverts to her barbaric life of the past?

∾

Was I afraid?

      Not a bit. I am a natural child
of the broad highway. I have had experiences enough
that would make Jack London and other reputed silk-gloved,
soft-handed wanderers sit up and wonder.

"A. No 1," the famous tramp, whose moniker decorates
every water tank in any town of consequence, is a friend of mine.

∾

from Nervous and Mental Diseases, *American Medical Association, 1922*

Psychopathy: Characterized by marked egotism, impulsiveness, poor judgment, nonconformity to ethical and social standards, and inability to adjust to or profit by discipline. Defect in volition not only makes it difficult to concentrate but also almost impossible to hold to one course of action long enough to succeed. Hence, many become industrial misfits, loafers, beggars, and paupers. The combination of this quality with an unusually strong desire to travel produces the hobo and the vagabond.

∾

I never had much trouble except in Oskaloosa.
They tried to make me work a rock pile.
The women saved me from such a fate.

I am willing to work—I have a knack
for telegraphy and can wait tables.

Someday I may settle down, but not
while youth lasts. It is too much fun traveling,
especially when one can steal rides.

Postcard

Union Stock Yards, Exchange Buildings and Cattle Pens, Chicago

The river in my heart
is parched and dry.

It packs its bags, leaves
its keys in the door.

Once it was a braid.
It was ravel and rope.

It folds and unfolds.
Now it churns up its banks.

It spits out the trees.
The river gathers its skirts.

It has no time for me.
When I open my mouth

it is hook and plunge,
snag on my sleeve. It dives

through my chest
because I am a marsh

and my breath is clotted
with weeds. The river

is fingering bolts of cotton.
It steers around stones.

Once it lapped
against roofs, curtains

blew into its oars, but now
the river is split and tear,

rise and sheer.
It won't come undone.

If I'm lucky, it will teach me
how to breathe.

Dictionary

All Tramps Sent Free
Atchison, Topeka & Santa Fe Railroad

Axle Swinging/Holding the Lady Down
lying on rods under moving train

Battleship
steel coal car with dump bottom

Cut Out/Ditch
drop off freight car

Deck
ride on top of car

Flip
hop off moving train

Floater
order by judge to get out of town

Gondola/Gonnie
shallow uncovered car

Johnnie O'Brien/Side-Door Pullman
boxcar

Clyde Dixon (V)

When she came to the door, asked if there were any chores,
did they invite her in, offer something to eat, or speak only

through the screen? They could wash her clothes—maybe an hour
to fill the tub—how much soda would it take?—then the ringer,

then the line—what would she wear, one of their dresses,
something old, from one of the boys, would that mean a place

in the loft or just till the damp wore off, *thank you,* she's
on her way— Did they need help with the children or carding,

wood for the fire, she sees you're making soap in the yard—
Pump some water, here's a biscuit, how long could she live

off a stolen spoon?— Did they still have the scarf
the woman left? *A present,* she said, *you were so kind.*

What did they want to know? *Hoe the garden.*
Mind the stove. What's it like on the high-wire?

Newsbreaks

In the Jefferson Market Court Miss Gertrude Williams was so frank about her exploits as a boy-tramp that the magistrate hesitated about sending her to the penitentiary. Her language was such a remarkable mixture of good English, Bowery slang, and terms picked up on the road that the magistrate was amazed. He finally committed her to the care of Miss Deschard, the probation officer.

~

There has not been found a satisfactory method for handling scarlet women, who are in fact female tramps. Even if all the hundreds of immoral women were captured, there would be no public institutions large enough to hold them. Development of the suffragette industry.

~

So much maudlin stuff has been written about the hobo by writers with socialistic views that many otherwise well-balanced people have become possessed of the idea that the hobo is usually some poor fellow driven to the wall by the pressure of unfair social conditions. But men with full knowledge of the crimes committed by these vile beasts (and most of these hobos are) are nauseated by the tolerance in which they are held. If the well-meaning people who have been "taken in" by this class of literature knew of the cases of rape of lone women and crimes so heinous they cannot be described, their opinion of the innocent, hard-luck-story-telling hobo would change.

The Sioux City police have arrested Alice Whalen three times during the last seven days. Her principal act is vagrancy, evidenced by her predilection for sleeping in the weeds.

Ganging

Greta Sorensen

Men on the road never have a woman,

                    and when there is a woman

they come around every time.

                  It ain't the looks of me.

Once on the road a man attacked me on a boxcar. He was the watchman

in the yards.

         He said he would hit me in the head if I didn't give in.

I fought him but he took me by the neck and threw me on the floor.

Another time on a lumber car—I went to sleep.

When I awoke a man was putting his blanket over me.

                        I told him to stop.

A man said to me if you don't give in, you have no business on the road.

He said it was his car

         [*evidently the boxcar*]

                  and he would put me off.

[*Were you ever ganged?*]

          No, no ganging.

There would always be a man or so who would protect me.

[*How did you avoid pregnancy on the road?*]

                  I am sterile.

The doctors said after my operation I would always be sterile.

[*Were you ever diseased?*]

         No, never.

              The men were all clean.

I am not afraid of them.

       [*But*]

          there is always a certain fear.

Postcard

Acres of Cotton, Muskogee, Oklahoma

The ghosts of horses
shudder
in their stalls

and the stars
stare blankly at the moon.
Light on the snow,

light
on the fields, I cannot
see my breath.

Even the trees
turn their backs, the sky
out of order,

no one can tell me
where I am—
Do not say I am stutter,

shaft, and flame.
I am a board
scraped clean, a blade

of clouds, a tin
of lies. Do not tell me
I do not blaze.

Clyde Dixon (VI)

What did she want and did she find it? Was it more
than a job: a roar in the ears, mountains she'll never

reach, or was it the ability to move, her life
a horse too wild to ride, a squeeze of the thigh, slight twist

of the heel— Not coneflowers, not switch-grass,
not a river slowing or a ball on a wheel—she had to learn

how to disappear, like starlings, like sparrows,
ubiquitous, invisible, except when they're not,

those evenings when they might swoop over stubbed fields,
updraft and swell, move out in waves, and their tinny wings

are leaves, are hours that shake, a crest of cottonwoods
and briars, so when a girl walks home from school,

claps her hands, it's jangle and scatter, the wind blows
through, next thing she knows—she's gone.

The Ballad of Sal Harper

Frisco Pete

When I saw this girl lam into my boxcar,
you can bet your hide I thought I'd get a break.

I said, *Hey, girlie, if you want company they's plenty here.*

The kid pretty near fainted when she saw me,

but she tried to let on
she wasn't scared.

She set down near the door, tucked her skirt
under her ankles, acted like I was somebody she knowed all her life.

Hello there, old-timer, she said.

Maybe that didn't make me feel good.

Anybody wise could see I was just an ordinary monkey on the bum.

I edged up to the kid and started makin' love, but she didn't see it that way,

so I started tellin' her what a tough time she was goin' to run into
before she got through.

Come to find out, she was scared as hell,
but she wasn't goin' back.

She got off the train at the next stop and said she'd stick there
long enough to get somethin' to eat.

I offered to hustle some chuck,
but not a chance.

I got me a feed, piled on when the train come
to the other end of the yards.

It was dark by that time.

Inside there was a flock of stiffs. Most of' 'em seemed like home guards
out for an airin'. One of 'em says,

Where you goin', fella?
I told him I'd come in on the train,

and another one says,
Maybe he knows the girl.

And back in one corner I heard
a kind of breakin' voice say, *Is that you, Pete?*

and I knowed
it was Sal Harper.

Yeh, it's me, I said;

and the girl said,
Well, for God's sake, do something.

But there wasn't anything
I figured I could do, and the train was hittin' up by that time,
so I just stood still.

Later, the train slowed up a little,
and you should a seen the way them guys tumbled out of that car.
I wasn't lookin' for no trouble, and I piled out with 'em,
right smack into the dark.

You see that girl over there?
She looked like her, in blue.

47

High-Wire: Nell Hale

When she left her husband, when she first made her way
from St. Joseph to Omaha to Chicago to Oak Grove,

what made her think she could go on? She had to know
railroads, how they worked, and the nuns at school who trekked

from St. Cloud one year after Kansas became a state,
they must have told the girls about the wind and the sun,

how they were ferried across the Missouri, their wagons, lanterns
swinging along shore. She never says what her husband did,

but St. Joseph was home to "eleven railroads, 170 factories,
thirteen miles of the best paved streets, and (for a while)

the largest stockyards in the West." She changed her name
from Nell Hale to Nell Cruise, became whoever she needed to be

so a farmer's wife might offer her scraps, the Ladies' Benevolent Society
would give her clothes: once a double-breasted coat of biased gores,

once a black dress, a train of cotton voile. How when she was
learning math and geography, she would have plotted the journey

to those very rooms. *Long Beach, Logansport, Albuquerque,
Canby*— How Marcus J. Barone told the papers he met her

in Colorado, before Paradise Gorge, and while the train rattled
and hummed, while it was still in motion and the canyon dropped

and the sky slid, a group of men pushed her out the door— *Quapaw,
Cincinnati, Casa Grande, L.A.*— How long did she lie by the river

until she came to, how long did she stay after, was there a moon
or was it just rocks, did she follow the walls till they sloped

to the plain or did she scramble up to the track, catch her balance,
a high-wire act, her sequined body water in light, or did she

dust her skirt, wipe her face, did she question, she had
to question what she was doing— Which way did she go?

Clyde Dixon (VII)

What exactly could she say? She didn't want
to upset her mother, or did she, maybe one day

she was hoping to go home— Did she think
her letter would catch up with her sister? How long

would it take? Did she sell off the piano, her father's tools,
get a cousin to take her in, or did she find some way to stay,

a man to marry, put the farm in his name?
If the letter found her, what would she think?

Tell the truth and she'll worry you're a whore, leave it out
and she might think the same. All she could say is,

I'm going to Chicago/Kansas City/Topeka/St. Paul.
I'm still hoping/looking/trying for a place, meaning,

I lay in the grass with the brakeman to stay on the train.
I demanded water so I could wash myself clean.

Newsbreaks

Show me a "lady hobo" and I'll show you an angular, flint-eyed, masculine travesty upon her sex.

❧

Susan Shelley of York Springs, Pa., made her way to Chicago, Ill., riding in true hobo style and clad in male attire. She delighted in having the police on her trail and seemed to get great enjoyment out of their peremptory orders to move on to another town.

❧

It is manifest folly to turn loose the female tramp after she has served a term in the House of Correction, for of course she can only go back to her old associations. But in a new home, with a chance to reform in a remote region, she might become a useful member of society.

❧

Samuel Chambers and George Collins, the two Negroes convicted of outraging Kate Smith near Middletown, Del., August 15 last, were hanged today. The woman was a tramp and in company with James Clegg.

Since conviction Clegg has declared that his testimony was false. He has been arrested for perjury. He claims Miss Smith willingly laid down with the men, but after they refused to pay the agreed-upon sum, she accused them of an attack and enlisted his help with the police.

Notwithstanding these declarations, the governor was deaf to appeals for pardon or reprieve.

∾

The evolution from horizontality to verticality was more difficult for females than it was for males. Woman might be physiologically truer to herself if she went about always on all fours.

Prodigal: Greta Sorensen

If she stepped onto a truss, looked down, between her feet, if she studied the
rocks, the river's split and pull, and looked into the trees, did they drag like
drapes or blow like horses along the road, how far back did the cottonwoods
grow, and if she hid in a culvert, did she crouch till dark, who did she follow,
who followed her, did she want bread, did she want salt, she counted the
ties, how far did she go, did she hear the men straightening the tracks,
she heard the rhythm of their rods, did she eat cattail, fireweed, she was
unrecognizable, *Lula, Lula, don't you know,* she swelled like a river, she swept
everything in, curtains and chairs, a trail of mud and mold on the walls, and
that feeling of falling, of being trapped in a well, she was grabbed by the hair,
did it make her want to be without a body, leave it behind like a skirt on
the floor, be sinew and bone, be breath and flushed those times she couldn't
stand her own skin, and did she think the water might hold her in its shift
and swirl, fit an end to the story like a dressmaker's form, as if what's left
is that space, the air in the cage, and she's night threatening rain, a cloud
charged with light, a swoop of smoke and hooves.

HIKING NELL

—The Noted Female Tramp—
Tells Local Women Why She Does It

REPORTER:
Macon, Mo.—A fugitive from the State Insane Asylum at Little Rock,
chased out of Moberly under suspicion she was the "woman in black,"

Hiking Nell, the famed woman tramp hit town one moonshiny night
and hunted up her old friend Fire Chief Charles Jones, for a shakedown
in the city lockup, which is one part of the engine house.

The woman, who has wandered from coast to coast,

                                                       traveling 25 years
to the land of Nowhere,
                        admitted she was approaching the end of her long, long trail.

WOMAN:
You're not going to die, are you Nell?

NELL CRUISE:
No, I've been too many times near old Grim to be afraid of him.

REPORTER:
Nell wouldn't have made a hit on the front pages of a popular magazine this trip.
She wouldn't take a prize at a beauty show,
                                    but looks are the least of her worries.

For the first time in her long tramping career, "Hiking Nell" is lonesome!
She meets up with no comrades of the road as in the good old days.
The hobos have vanished.

NELL CRUISE:
Gone to work!

WOMAN:
Where do you sleep of nights?

NELL CRUISE:
(*Laughs.*)
Outdoors most generally—in straw stacks, barns, haylofts,
switch shanties, lots of places.

Once they gave me a feather bed in a farmhouse,

                                           but I couldn't sleep.
I took the quilt, climbed out the window.

REPORTER:
There are two other noted women wanderers yet on the road,
Nell said—Boxcar Anna and Gypsy Nell—

NELL CRUISE:
But they're not real tramps.
                             They'll ride in anything going their way.
I don't.

WOMAN:
How long were you in the asylum?

NELL CRUISE:
Three years, one month, and a day. It was a frame-up!

I'm no more crazy than you are, and they knew it.
And they got me in with a lot of people who didn't know
the difference between a bull pup and the multiplication table.

I got a case against somebody down there soon as I find a lawyer that's honest.

WOMAN:
Were you ever married?

NELL CRUISE:
Married? I should say I was. That's what made a tramp out of me.
Married for seven years. He just beat me up every day until I left.

That was twenty years ago. I have sure enjoyed myself.
Going from married life onto the road is like stepping from hell to heaven.

WOMAN:
The rough men ever bother you?

NELL CRUISE:
Just once—about a year ago. It was in Oregon.
A fool crook slugged me—see that dent in my head.
He thought I had money—the big stiff! I was laid out three days.

When I came to I thought I was in heaven.
                              Then I heard
one of those mule auto-horns braying outside and thought it was
the other place.
                    The doctor said I was an "interesting case,"
looked like he wanted to dissect me in the name of science.
So I hurried up getting well and moved along.
                              The Petes

REPORTER:
(burglars, yeggs, and road crooks generally)

NELL CRUISE:
never harmed me. They all knew me—I was on the level.

No, I never helped 'em—I never took a nickel that didn't belong to me.

What makes me tramp this way?
                                I don't know.
In the blood, I reckon, like folks who hunt the North Pole or train elephants
or go over the Falls in a barrel.
                                I've crossed the Rockies seven times,
don't want to play mahjong, do the foxtrot.

Clyde Dixon (VIII)

If she had gone to school, made it to sixth, maybe
eighth grade, what did she read? Not just *McGuffey's*

but Gypsy Breynton, Ragged Dick, Tattered Tom, did she find
"The Land of Nod," want the basket in "A Pirate Story," remember

the tramp who "stood and gazed" outside "A Railway Carriage,"
did she want her own island, make her own boat, have

her own forest, did she want to travel by balloon— She found
Palgrave's Golden Treasury, pored through its pages, stood

by the stove for recitation while her classmates stared
at their slates, the map on the wall. Dryden, Herbert,

Marvell, Vaughn. How far did she get with *Paradise Lost*?
What hath night to do with sleep? What though the field be lost?

Wasn't she taught to venture down? What did she find?
O heavenly Muse. Why should to know mean to fall?

Dictionary

Bazoo
mouth

Catch a Westbound
die

Chuck a Dummy
fake a fainting spell

Hi-Line
Great Northern Railroad

Home Guard
local worker

Ice Palace
brothel with mirrors

Meg
penny

O.P.C.
other people's cigarettes

Take the Shortline
commit suicide

Wing/Wingy
rider who lost an arm

Clyde Dixon (IX)

It depends: did she get on early morning or sometime
at night, how much light reached into the car, were there

men, stacked crates, lumber or coal or a load of grain
she could let herself sink in? Did she know anyone

who had tried this before? She talked, played cards,
did she want to enter a tunnel of blue leaves, then clattering

wet bricks, a stench that won't end, stop listening
to the shuffling on top, men tying themselves in, the grips

and the rungs— She listened for work, the police, picking
peaches, tobacco, a spot at one of the looms, she shut

enough fear down her throat she could slip between cars,
jostle and jog, the engine passed, did she heave herself in,

that stretch in the back when her feet left the ground, all
the shouting, the weird silence, then the leap and low trill—

Family Secrets and Recessive Genes

A few days ago a woman who claimed
to be one of the Johnstown sufferers
appeared in San Bernardino.
A considerable sum was raised,
and she was sent to Los Angeles.
It is now supposed that the woman
was none other than the famous tramp Mae Watson,
who travels from one end of the country
to the other, a few days here, a few days there,
never satisfied to remain, making her home
wherever chance may throw her. She was born
in South Carolina, the daughter of one
of the most prominent families. She was

A BEAUTIFUL GIRL

of that Southern type which poets rave about.
Her parents, proud of their only daughter,
lavished money on her education,
provided her with the best masters.
On a neighboring plantation lived
a bachelor, handsome, brave, intelligent.
It was but natural they should fall in love.
There were no objections to the match,
and marriage followed. The planter was proud of

HIS BRILLIANT WIFE

and after an extended bridal tour
they settled down. Everything passed smoothly,
the loving wife doting on the fond husband,
he finding pleasure in her happiness.
By and by a bond came and he was overjoyed
at the advent of an heir. But his joy
was short-lived. A few weeks passed

and the planter wore a haggard look.
His visits to her sick chamber became fewer. The

DENOUEMENT CAME AT LAST

when the wife's father was told to take
his daughter home. The father demanded
an explanation. The husband took him
to see the heir. It had black, kinky hair,
a dark, olive-hued complexion. It was
a Negro baby. The father joined the husband
in his maledictions at the young mother
for her supposed infidelity and refused
to receive her in his home. She pleaded
she was honest. She was cast from the door.
She finally wandered to New Orleans,
which before the war was a perfect

WHIRL OF EXCITEMENT.

To drown her sorrow, she plunged into
a vortex of depravity. A few years later
the aged father died, but on his deathbed
he sent for a notary and made a statement
that there was Negro blood in his veins,
but he was too proud to save his daughter
and flung her out into the world.
The husband at once went to New Orleans
to reclaim his wife, but she was beyond
redemption. The woman continued

HER MAD CAREER

and dove deeper into her life of sin
until worn out and she no longer attracted

attention. It was then, under the name
Mae Watson, she began traveling from ocean
to ocean, the gulf to the lakes, from one part
of the country to another. She treads
her way, existing as best she can.
She will probably live in Los Angeles
a few days and then suddenly
disappear, going, no one knows where,
but continuing her endless journey.

.

Postcard

Looking north on Washington Avenue, Ogden, Utah

What I'm trying to say is it may come to this:
having made a series of choices that may or may not
have been yours, having heard not one but what you swear

is every single door close, you may find yourself in a field
that, in retrospect, might be considered (from a distance)
pretty, crawling through the grass on all fours. It's okay.

You'll want soap, you'll want to cut off what's left
of your hair. If you have a brush, you'll want
to scrub off your skin. I didn't want that either,

didn't know my life had become one strand
of an unnamable vine that fools you with flowers
that trumpet nothing but noise. You wait tables,

then you don't. You spin plates like an acrobat.
You flutter your fans. Children run up to the tracks,
they wave as you pass. Women in town turn slightly,

find reasons to look in their bags. You might want to set
the whole field on fire, watch it burn like pages ripped
from a book. Your feet will stick to the ground,

it will take everything in you to let out a sound, but I will
wash your hair, rinse your clothes, find a way to mend your collar
and your cuff. I will hold you while you sleep. We will eat

berries off a tree, dandelion leaves, pennycress seeds, and then,
when we are full and drunk like birds, swallows heading
into a dive, we will wade through the grass, we will carry sticks

and pine needles if we can find them—it doesn't matter
who's there—we'll stand in the center of the field on what
someone might call *a beautiful day*, and I will hand you the match.

Paradise Lost

Greta Sorensen

Yes, I'm real happy on the road.
                              I don't want any assaults—outside of that,
I've been happy.

                    [*What is the most pleasant thing that happened to you?*]
When I was hungry and someone gave me something to eat.

[*Anything else?*]
                    It is pleasant to go from town to town.

[*What is the toughest experience you've had?*]
                                        When I can't find any water
and want to get clean.
                    When I am pushed, I go to a house and ask if I can wash.

[*What is the most dangerous thing on the road?*]
                                        People don't realize the dangers
in falling off trains and how the cars can throw you.

                                   [*Did you ever hop a train*
while in motion?]
                    Twice. A man grabbed me each time and pulled me on.

[*Can you make it in a boxcar by yourself?*]
                                   I can jump, but it's hard
to push the doors back. A girl mighty near needs a man do that. Even men get help.

[*Weren't you afraid of so many men close at night?*]
                                        Some men protect me—
like some countries have a protectorate.

                                   [*Do you think you have lost anything mentally*
or physically living this way?]
                    No, I think it has been more of a gain.

My mind is more developed.

[*What did you do with all the time you had on the road?*]
We talked mostly.

[*What else?*]
Read.

[*Read what?*]
Books.

[*What books?*]
The Bible. Poems.

[*What poems?*]
Paradise Lost—

Clyde Dixon (X)

She spent her days at Marshall Field's, Carson Pirie Scott,
asking the girls to show her ribbons and gloves, counters-full

of trimmings she couldn't afford, knowing they wouldn't
throw her out. She looked for the Salvation Army girls,

their long black capes, "SLUM" down their sash, said she was high,
afraid of a man, sang about Jesus for a bed for the night—

Or was her best bet a dance hall, a boxing match, ask a man
to pay for a lantern show, the Opera House— *The Air Ship* was playing,

"A Musical Farce Comedy," "Full of Fun"—a boat with sails and wheels
and a giant jury-rigged balloon, stars on the ceiling, bathing beauties

on the bow, everyone holding onto their hats, they're headed
for the Klondike, the professor shouting, *We're going to strike it rich,*

as the tramp steps out of her rags, a low evening gown, and from the sky
raises her arm over the house and begins to sing chansonettes.

All My Life

Clyde Dixon

Most everybody took me for a boy.

I always dressed neat and kept myself
clean. That helped.

                I tried milking cows,
doing chores.

              Once a brakeman struck me
when I refused to give him a dollar to ride
one of his dirty cars, and once I came near
being caught.

             I was standing in front
of a millinery store, admiring the pretty hats

when a man came past, saw me, came to my side
and said, "How'd you like one of those hats,
dear?"

           I ran down the street.

                    I was homesick
for a while, but I knew my folks would not
let me back, so I tried to forget.

I have slept in barns, good hotels.
I have slept in open fields on summer nights.

Am I going back?

I may as well. You don't think
I could keep this up all my life?

Missouri State Hospital No. 4: Nell Cruise

July 9, 1944

Her death certificate says the immediate cause
was pneumonia—it lasted thirty-three days after a fall.

She'd been there twelve years, six months, seven days,
before that St. Louis City Sanitarium, before that

who knows—if she somehow escaped from Williamsburg,
lifting the latch at the end of the hall, if she went straight

to Florida or if she wanted to go back to where she was born
and found herself where the rail yard met the Mississippi,

looking up at the barrel-vaulted ceiling in the depot's Grand Hall.
There's no public record that says why she was committed

or what her treatment was or why she was kept so long.
The hospital was overcrowded—when she died at least

600 more people than when she came, 200 lobotomies in three years,
if it was *Life*'s "Bedlam" with people restrained and lying

on the floor or a modern hospital with a dairy barn and cannery,
long paths, "villas," a theater/bowling alley and salon—

How were her days? When she came, did she check in her things,
shelves with suitcases and satchels, trunks with wing-tipped

and kitten-heeled shoes, did she hand in her clothes for calico or chintz,
a dress the women made because work, along with water,

was part of the cure—two seams, an elastic waist, a wide hem—
it couldn't have hung past her knees—mosaic white florals,

contrasting necks—turquois, carnelian, melon—easy to slip on, colors
so vigorously alive, and someone saying, "Look, this one suits you,

it sets off your eyes/your hair/your skin." How long did she have
that dress? Who was there when they lowered her down?

Postcard

Spokane, Portland & Seattle Railway, Columbia River Bridge

The horse steps
to the fence.

Its nostrils
open and close.

It dips its head
slowly. It wants me

to put my hand
on its star.

I have nothing
to give. It doesn't

understand—
if I touched it,

it would mean
I was here.

NOTES

"Tramp" comes from the Middle German word *trampen*—to stamp, walk heavily. It referred to the steady sound of working animals as well as the sudden, heavy, downward strike of a foot. During the romantic period, the word began to be used for a long, tiring walk, often during a search for work, and for the vagabonds who took them. It wasn't until the early twentieth century that "tramp" became synonymous with a sexually active woman. It probably stems from the fact that many female tramps exchanged sex for food and shelter while on the road. Because of the lack of records and the nature of homelessness, historians do not know how many people tramped or for how long. Contemporary estimates during the late nineteenth and early twentieth centuries range in the low millions; the percentage of women is unknown, though one guess during the Depression was 5 to 10 percent of the overall tramping population.

"A Man Mistreated Ada Jones and She Is Seeking Him" is based on "Girl Hobo Has a Purpose," *Kansas City Star*, August 25, 1911. In this poem and the other documentary pieces, I have worked to maintain the original voices while reshaping the texts and tightening the language, occasionally changing names and places and adding bits of information that would have been understood by a contemporary audience.

"Bodies of Evidence (I)" is based on: "Woman Tramp Murdered," *Springfield Republican*, October 30, 1902; "'Box Car Lulu' Flits into City," *Omaha World Herald*, September 6, 1901; "'Wish I Was a Boy' Cries a Girl Tramp," *Pawtucket Times*, July 25, 1914; "Why Women Become Hobos," Walter C. Reckless, *American Mercury*, February 1934.

"Newsbreaks" (Part 1): Newspapers used to print long columns of "newsbreaks," or breaking news. Running anywhere from a sentence to a couple of paragraphs, they covered everything from a lost cow and readers' vacation plans to matters of regional and national importance. These are based on: "Hail, the Lady Hobo, Latest Suffragette!" *Los Angeles Times*, March 2, 1913; "Girl Arrested after Hold-Up," *Los Angeles Times*, July 24, 1922; Editorial, *Fort Worth Star-Telegram*, August 14, 1916.

"Hiking Nell Faces the August Majesty of the Law" and the other Hiking Nell pieces are based on "Woman Tramp in Court," *Pasco Express*, March 4, 1909; "Woman of Education Is Tramp by Choice," *Fort Worth Star-Telegram*, May 29, 1910; "Hiking Nell," *Utica Saturday Globe*, July 27, 1920; and the many articles about her that appeared over the years.

During the late nineteenth and early twentieth centuries, men and women participated in long-distance walking-wagers. Betting thousands of dollars, gamblers weighed in on whether a particular "pedestrian" could walk a set distance in a certain amount of time. The pedestrians stood to make up to $10,000 walking indoor tracks or covering great distances. The first man to make such a walk was Edward Payson Weston, when he walked from Portland, Maine, to Chicago in twenty-six days. Female "pedestriennes" came from poor and working-class backgrounds and hoped to change their situations with freshly won cash. The press looked upon them with a mixture of admiration and contempt.

"Reenie Patterson Talks to the Press about Her Time on the Road" is based on *Riding the Rails*, by Michael Uys and Lexy Lovell, *PBS: American Experience*, 1998, and *Boy and Girl Tramps of America*, by Thomas Minehan (New York: Farrar and Rinehart, 1934).

"Bodies of Evidence (II)" is based on: "A Female Tramp Killed," *Dodge City Times*, August 30, 1879; "Girl Hobo Leaves Social Life for Call of the Wild," *Philadelphia Inquirer*, April 29, 1922; "The Female Tramp," *Los Angeles Times*, November 30, 1894; "Life of a Woman Tramp," *Bismarck Daily Tribune*, February 21, 1897; "A Night in the Women's City Lodging House," *Idaho Statesman*, November 19, 1911; "Suffragist War Worker Who Walked Here from California Dies of 'Flu,'" *Washington Times*, October 24, 1918.

For the wandering poor who did not want to sleep outside or at a religious poorhouse (which meant mandatory attendance at services and prayers), local jails often provided shelter for the night. The New York Municipal Lodging House, 432 East 25th Street, was built in 1909. It had 964 beds, 164 of which were reserved for women and children. Men had to work five hours a day to earn their keep. The city eventually built two annexes, one at Pier Seventy-Three at 25th Street and the other at the old Brooklyn ferry terminal building at 39th Street, adding nearly five thousand beds. *Ripley's Believe It or Not!* called Annex Number One, which was capable of housing three thousand people, the "largest bedroom in the world." Lodgers received medical and dental exams as well as three meals a day. The Municipal Lodging House came down in 1949 to make way for the new Veterans Administration Hospital, which still stands.

"Diagnostics" is based on "Hazel Davis, Girl Tramp, Beating Way East, Is Taken from Train at Midnight and Sent to Jail," *Colorado Springs Gazette*, November 9, 1912.

"Newsbreaks" (Part 2) is based on: "Pretty Girl Hobo in Boy's Clothes," *Pawtucket Times*, August 26, 1908; "Findings of Vice Board Defended," *Oregonian*, September 2, 1912, and "Proving It's Dangerous to Be Alive," *Idaho Statesman*, September 26, 1911; "A Female Tramp," *Omaha World Herald*, July 29, 1902; "New Ideals in Police Administration," *B&O Employees Magazine*, vol. 3, 1914.

"Ganging" and "Paradise Lost" are based on "Why Women Become Hobos," Walter C. Reckless, *American Mercury*, February 1934. Compulsory sterilization statutes first appeared in the United States in 1907. They were based on Harry Laughlin's 1914 "Model Eugenical Sterilization Law," which authorized the forced sterilization of the "feebleminded, insane, criminalistic, epileptic, inebriate, diseased, blind, deaf, deformed, and dependent," including "orphans, ne'er-do-wells, tramps, the homeless, and paupers." By the mid-1970s, over 60,000 Americans had been involuntarily sterilized.

"The Ballad of Sal Harper" is based on "Lady Hobos," Samuel Elam, *New Republic*, January 1, 1930.

"Newsbreaks" (Part 3) is based on: "Lady Vagabonds," Cliff Maxwell, *Scribner's*, March 1929; "An Unsophisticated Hobo," *Conductor and Brakeman Magazine*, 1901; "An Anatomical Vindication of the Straight Front Corset," *Current Literature*, February 1910; "Black Friday, Two Colored Men Hanged," *Burlington Daily Hawkeye*, March 23, 1878; "Vagrant Population," *Philadelphia North American*, February 7, 1876.

"Hiking Nell" and "Missouri State Hospital No. 4: Nell Cruise": At the turn of the century, women could be declared insane and institutionalized for dozens of reasons that would not be accepted today. They included abortion, asthma, childbirth, domestic trouble, egotism, epilepsy, female trouble, grief, imaginary female trouble, inability to speak English, loss of property, marriage of son, menopause, novel reading, nymphomania, overexertion (physical or mental), politics, religious disagreement, religious excitement, and the use of abusive language. When Nell Hale was committed by a judge to the Virginia Hospital for the Insane in 1925, the *Richmond Times-Dispatch* expressed disbelief in her story about walking across the United States, suggesting it was evidence of her mental instability.

"Family Secrets and Recessive Genes" is based on "A Strange Story," *San Jose Evening News*, July 31, 1889.

"All My Life" is based on "Girl Hobo," *Tulsa World*, November 16, 1911.

ACKNOWLEDGMENTS

Grateful acknowledgment is made to the editors of the following journals for first publishing these poems, sometimes under slightly different titles:

Cincinnati Review: "Postcard: Monongahela R.R. Passenger and Freight Station, West Side, Morgantown, W.Va." and "Postcard: Spokane, Portland, and Seattle Railway, Columbia River Bridge"

Colorado Review: "Postcard: Three Bridges on Ohio River between East Liverpool and Steubenville, Ohio" and "Postcard: Union Pacific Transfer Depot, Council Bluffs, Iowa"

Fledgling Rag: "Postcard: Acres of Cotton, Muskogee, Oklahoma," "Postcard: Union Stock Yards, Exchange Buildings and Cattle Pens, Chicago," and "Thinking of Heaven: Greta Sorensen"

Greensboro Review: "Postcard: Looking North on Washington Avenue, Ogden, Utah"

Harvard Review: "Clyde Dixon," poems I–X

Pleiades: "Bodies of Evidence (I)," "Bodies of Evidence (II)," and "Diagnostics"

Poetry Northwest: "High-Wire," "Hiking Nell Faces the August Majesty of the Law," "Jail House: Interview," and "On the Origins of Trampdom"

Puerto del Sol: "A Man Mistreated Ada Jones and She Is Seeking Him" and "Reenie Patterson Talks to the Press about Her Time on the Road"

Southern Review: "Paradise Lost" and "Prodigal: Greta Sorensen"

Sou'wester: "In Her Other Life: Greta Sorensen"

Yew: "All My Life" and "The Ballad of Sal Harper"

Special thanks to Nadia Colburn, Melissa Dickey, Barbara Fischer, Molly Sutton Kiefer, Matthew Olshan, Michele Osherow, Patrick Phillips, Stanley Plumly, Martha Silano, and Leah Souffrant for their feedback and friendship; to my parents, brother, friends, and the mamas for their support; to The Studios of Key West for a residency that gave me time to revise; to Michael Uys and Lexy Lovell for permission to use excerpts from their film, *Riding the Rails*; and to MaryKatherine Callaway, Ava Leavell Haymon, and everyone at LSU Press. To Kirk, Katie, Andrew, and Erik—all my love.